The sayings of
Zen Buddhism

The sayings of
Zen Buddhism

Peaceful reflections on life

SIRIUS

SIRIUS

This edition published in 2019 by Sirius Publishing, a division of
Arcturus Publishing Limited,
26/27 Bickels Yard, 151–153 Bermondsey Street,
London SE1 3HA

ISBN: 978-1-78950-009-7
AD006891UK

Printed in China

CONTENTS

INTRODUCTION

The wisdom of the great figures of Zen
– Chinese masters, Japanese monks and
inspirational poets – is contained in this
collection of daily reflections. Their words
convey the spirit of Zen, an indefinable
essence which defies words.

The origins of Buddhism

It should not be forgotten that Zen is first
and foremost a branch of Buddhism.
This may seem obvious, but without directly relating Zen to its primary source,
the teachings of the Buddha, we would end up merely discussing its peculiarities
and not its fundamental inspiration. In turn, by considering the Buddha we must
also take into account his own philosophical background and cultural context.

It has often been argued that Buddhism is a reinterpretation of the teachings
of the Veda; that the Buddha arrived at it after a blinding insight into the central
truths of the Upanishads. The Buddha's concern was not with the workings of society
and the nature of an individual's destiny, but with universality. His teaching went
straight to the heart of self-realization. He became aware that reality was not to be
discovered through an involvement with all things separate, but through a dissolution
of separation. In this respect, he was acting entirely according to Vedic tradition.
Seeking the way of liberation, he followed *rishi*, the path of the forest. He abandoned
his worldly role and stepped outside the structure of the Hindu caste system.

The setting aside of caste distinctions marks a formal rejection of the ways in which identity is established within societies. No longer are there sons, husbands, fathers or householders. By abandoning these and all the other conventional ways of creating an identity, we are led to the recognition that we are, in truth, 'no-thing'. As far as the individual is concerned there is no self, for all sense of self-identity is 'blown away' in the moment of realization.

Out of the Buddha's awakening (*bodhi*) arose statements such as:

> *By the All-awakening One, fore-knowing, thoroughly knowing*
> *every world, opened is the door of the deathless;*
> *when* nirvana *is reached, there is security.*
> *There are the ten qualities which* nirvana *shares with space.*
> *Neither is born, grows old, dies, passes away or is reborn;*
> *both are unconquerable, cannot be stolen, are unsupported,*
> *and are unobstructed and infinite.*

The Buddha sat in meditation under the Bodhi Tree for seven weeks, aware that *nirvana* transcended all words. He pondered how he might deliver a teaching that allowed for their shortcomings and how they could act as an obstacle to self-realization. One could never argue that the Buddhist tradition lacks words – quite the opposite – but doctrine has always been of secondary importance to experiencing truth directly.

Mahayana Buddhism appears in China

When different philosophies meet, the exchange of ideas can produce long-lasting results. It is uncertain exactly when Mahayana Buddhism first appeared in China. According to one popular story, Bodhidharma, an Indian Buddhist master, arrived in China at some point during the last half of the 5th and first half of the 6th century. His message was:

> *Not relying on the words and letters, Teachings are transmitted*
> *outside the Scriptures; Pointing directly into one's mind, then one*
> *can see into his own nature and attains Buddhahood.*

This radical approach to teaching came from the Buddha himself. One day, instead of teaching in words, he merely held up a flower. Mahakasyapa, one of his disciples, smiled. The Buddha said: 'Today, I gave a silent teaching and Mahakasyapa alone understood it.'

This simple and spontaneous approach is very much part of the spirit of Zen. Direct pointing provides blessed relief from the contortions of the mind. It also indicates that the mind itself has to be transcended on the path to realization. The Buddha tells us that the self is not the mind, for the mind, too, must be 'blown away' in the quest for unity. Despite the immediacy of the approach adopted by

Zen, however, one of the ways in which Buddhism spread through China was by studying the great Indian texts.

The Mahayana Buddhist *Vimalakirti Sutra*, for example, has been of lasting importance. This text converted Seng-Chao, a notable Taoist scholar, to Buddhism. He became the pupil of the Indian monk Kumarajiva, who translated many of the Buddhist texts between the years 384 and 413, thereby making them available to the Chinese. Before becoming a student of Kumarajiva, Seng-Chao was a scribe of Taoist philosophy, and it was out of the meeting of these two traditions that Zen arose.

Embedded within the *Vimalakirti Sutra* is the idea of simple service as a way to emancipation. There is also the acknowledgement that words will only take you part of the way.

Our message will reach people simply because it is true!
There will come a time when many will no longer need words, but will be beyond words. We must all strive to go beyond the words, because words can be clung to, and we should not cling to things. Understand that the words of the Buddha are like a raft built to cross a river: when its purpose is completed, it must be left behind if we are to travel further!

Buddhism and Taoism

What was it about Buddhism that appealed to a scholar like Seng-Chao and many others who were steeped in Chinese philosophy? Part of the answer must lie in the nature of that philosophy. Taoist thinking is not by nature linear and logical. It doesn't rely on a body of theoretical abstractions but places value on the spontaneous insight derived from a direct understanding of the essence of life. This spontaneity is called *tzu-jan* (that which is naturally so). According to its masters, the *Tao*, which has been described as the indefinable process, or the Way, is beyond definition:

> *There was something vague before heaven and earth arose.*
> *How calm! How void! It stands alone, unchanging; it acts*
> *everywhere, untiring. It may be considered*
> *the mother of everything under heaven.*
> *I do not know its name but call it* Tao.
>
> Chang-Tzu

The relationship between the *Tao* and Creation is not one of lord and master, but of interpenetrating presences.

> *It loves and nourishes all things, but does not lord it over them.*
>
> Chang-Tzu

Tao is not a power that stands outside of ourselves, shaping the world to some pre-ordained plan. It is more of an inconceivable intelligence that, with spontaneous subtlety, forms the world out of love. The *Tao* does not create the world from without, but grows it from within. Such thinking doesn't demand that we stand outside of Creation and stamp a controlling influence on it. Instead it allows us to work spontaneously with it through intuitive understanding.

Both Buddhism and Taoism are philosophies of unity which hold that, in truth, there are not many, but only one. The vast and varied movements of the universe, both physical and subtle, are like bubbles on the surface of water because reality lies elsewhere. It is our task to discover that unity, to connect with the undivided by shedding all those things we gather around us. It requires the discarding of both the physical and the conceptual worlds. We also need to cast aside self-identity.

> *When a man, abandoning the false and embracing the true, in singleness of thought practises the Entrance by Reason he finds that there is neither self nor other, that the masses and the worthies are of one essence, and he firmly holds on to this belief and never moves away therefrom.*

Bodhidharma

The Zen approach

In Buddhism and Taoism, our task is to step away from and rid ourselves of physical desire and conceptual thinking. We should avoid pursuing the forms of this world and should not try to grasp some kind of identity through a relationship with these forms. Instead we should sink back into the essence of things.

> *This mind-essence is variously characterized as something original, mysterious, mysteriously bright, illuminating, true, perfect, clear as a jewel, etc. It is not to be confused with our empirical mind, for it is not an object of intellectual discrimination.*

That is how Bodhidharma described mind-essence. But writing about it is one thing; experiencing it is another. Methods of meditation were developed which allowed for the dissolution of attachments. The term Zen clearly indicates the essential approach that was adopted, for *zen* and *ch'an* are the respective Japanese and Chinese renderings of the Sanskrit term *dhyana* (meaning contemplation or meditation). *Dhyana* has a specific meaning within Buddhism. It is the state of consciousness of a Buddha, one whose mind is free from the duality of subject and object, and from the belief that the distinct individuality of oneself and another thing is real. Reality is the 'suchness' (*Pali tathata*) of nature, or the world 'just as it is', free from any overlay of concepts.

The task is to abandon all forms of personal conceptualization and see the world 'just as it is'. Zen came about through the Chinese masters who devised and realized this way of seeing with an 'empty mind', devoid of grasping thoughts or feelings. This attitude is called 'no-mind' (*wu-hsin* in Chinese; *trishna* in Sanskrit). Thoughts arise in this state, but they pass without leaving any trace because there is no attempt to grasp them. Such freedom of mind cannot be attained by gradual practice; it must arise suddenly and spontaneously through direct and immediate 'insight into one's true nature' (*tun-wu* in Chinese; *satori* in Japanese).

Zen is not concerned, therefore, with building up a body of theory. Instead it communicates its understanding through 'direct pointing' (*chih-chih*), with the master answering philosophical or religious questions by direct and literal words or actions. The answer is the action just as it is, not what it represents. The responses arise directly out of what appear to be everyday affairs. Although there is little evidence that this approach appeared as a formal method before the Tang Dynasty (AD618–907), instant 'Awakening' in the midst of mundane affairs was a feature common to the early masters.

> *'What is Zen?' asked a monk.*
> *'Brick and stone'.*
> *'What is the Tao?'*
> *'A block of wood'.*

Zen students prepare for such responses with meditation (*za-zen* in Japanese). This practice clears the mind and eliminates all forms of conceptual thinking so that one is ready to receive a direct and intuitive understanding.

Mind-essence is immediate and found in all things. It is perceived by *prajna*: direct insight that is a kind of ignorance because it knows by not knowing. It follows, then, that true wisdom is not a body of concepts but a matter of direct illumination.

> *Outside teaching; apart from tradition.*
> *Not founded on words or letters.*
> *Pointing directly to the human mind.*
> *Seeing into one's nature and attaining Buddhahood.*

Suzuki

Experience, not words, is the central issue and this appreciation is essential to Zen.

> *My way is through mind-awakening.*
> *How can it be conveyed in words?*

The Wang Ling Record

Karma and *nirvana*

In the realization of unity, the fundamental duality that rules our experience of life dissolves. *Avidya* (ignorance) is rooted in this relationship, which is reinforced by words, the subtle products of the mind. Some Buddhists believe the very act of thinking proves that their existence is separate. The Buddha's Awakening laid bare the knowledge that separateness is only a seeming reality, and that clinging to this reality ties us to *samsara* (the circle of birth and death). This cycle is known as *karma* and we will go on experiencing its effects as long as we are identified with our relational state and persist in clinging to our seeming deeds. According to traditional teaching, the cycle is held in a dynamic structure of twelve causal links:

ignorance (*avidya*) > motivation (*samskara*) > individual consciousness > (*vijnana*) > name and form (*namarupa*) > the six senses (*shadayatans*) > sense stimulation (*sparsa*) > sense experience (*vedana*) > grasping (*trishna*) > possessiveness (*upadana*) > coming to be (*bhava*) > birth (*jati*) > old age and death (*jamarana*)

The Buddha insisted that we should step away from the wheel of life, full as it is of identifications, desires and disappointments. Instead we should:

> *Abandon the ways of confusion and darkness*
> *and live in the light of peace and harmony.*
> *[For] the cessation of craving successively leads to that*
> *of grasping, of becoming, of birth, of old age and death,*
> *of grief, lamentation, pain, sadness and despair.*

As the 'Sudden Enlightenment' School of Buddhism, Zen incorporates the belief that we can sidestep the karmic cycle in a moment through direct and immediate insight (*satori*):

> *One in All,*
> *All in One –*
> *If only this were realized,*
> *No more worry about you not being perfect.*
>
> The *Sutra* of Wei Leung

The final aim of Zen coincides with that of all of Buddhism – the achievement of *nirvana*. This state of bliss involves the extinguishing of all involvement with the wheel of *samsara* (the perpetual wandering in a cycle of rebirth) to discover the 'Great Self': the undivided universe. However, the Zen masters believed that *nirvana* was not to be discovered in some exalted mystical realm, but in the everyday.

The Buddha recalled an event in his childhood that took place just before he achieved enlightenment. He was watching his father ploughing in the shade of a rose-apple tree. The steady measure of the ox team and the play of sunlight and shade allowed him unexpected access to a state beyond that of the movement of life. Perhaps, therefore, enlightenment was not the subject of striving but was simple and natural. Maybe it was achieved by becoming aware of that which truly suffused all the mundane movements of life. Buddhahood is achieved through this awareness. This naturalness and simplicity is very much a mark of the Zen spirit:

> *He lives in equanimity, calmly and contentedly.*
> *He is free from all care, yet he acts naturally and reasonably.*
> *He neither strives to avoid delusion nor seeks after truth.*
> *He knows delusions as baseless and truth as himself.*
>
> The *Sutra* of Wei Leung

The main Zen sects

The Zen masters developed different techniques for achieving this immediacy and simplicity. There are two main sects of Zen: Rinzai Zen and Soto Zen. The Rinzai school was introduced into Japan in 1191 by the monk Eisai, who established monasteries at Kyoto and Kamakura. The Soto school was introduced in 1227 by Dogen, who established his monastery at Eiheiji. Soto concentrates on sitting meditation (*za-zen*), whereas Rinzai makes use of *za-zen* in conjunction with meditation on paradoxical statements (*koan*). In the Soto monasteries, *za-zen* practices are followed for many hours a day, with precise attention being paid to posture and breathing. This is all directed towards a state of concentration known as *Samadhi* (literally 'firmly fixed'). Correct concentration is the final step on the Buddha's Eight-fold Path. Its aim is *nirvana* – true peace achieved by ending 'all formations by the forsaking of every substratum of rebirth' and the extinction of greed, hate and delusion. This is the ultimate goal of all Buddhists.

The *Koan* system of the Rinzai school is based on a technique that was developed by Chinese masters. Students are expected to demonstrate their understanding of an incident by means of a direct, intuitive response that transcends conceptual thinking. The whole approach is designed to find freedom from logical mindsets and is considered to lead directly to mental awakening (*satori*). Great reliance is placed on encouraging doubt (*i-ching*), and the system seeks to challenge the ideas we hold about ourselves together with our relationship to the world:

About the koan, *you should single out the point where you have been in doubt all your life and put it upon your forehead. Is it a holy or a commonplace one? Is it an entity or a non-entity? Press your question to its very end. Do not be afraid of plunging yourself into a vacuity; find out what it is that cherishes the sense of fear. Is it a void or is it not?*

Tai-Hui

These training schools often employ manual labour in addition to meditative techniques, in an attempt to avoid being bound by the mind. As the Buddha-mind is to be found in everything, there is an emphasis on a connection with action rather than conceptual thinking, and with the direct vision of nature rather than an interpretation. This has exerted a profound influence on the arts in Japan. While Zen religious painting might avoid iconography, it portrays natural forms such as birds, grasses, rocks and mountains in a style that combines maximum technique with minimum deliberation.

> *There is here, not there.*
> *Infinity is before our eyes.*
>
> Seng T'san

This approach also affected poetry, calligraphy, gardening and architecture. It is at the heart of ceremonial tea drinking and has influenced the arts of fencing, archery and ju-jitsu. It is recognized as the essence behind everything.

> *O my good friends gathered here,*
> *If you desire to listen to the thunderous voice of the Way,*
> *Exhaust your words, empty your thoughts,*
> *For then you may come to recognize this One Essence.*
>
> Dai-o Kokushi

The Sayings of
Zen Buddhism

All beings by nature are Buddhas,
as ice by nature is water.
Apart from water, there is no ice;
Apart from beings, no Buddhas.

Take heed, do not squander your life.
If you want to travel the Way of Buddhas
and Zen masters, then expect nothing, seek
nothing and grasp nothing.
To escape from the world means that one's
mind is not concerned with the opinions
of the world.

Pursue not the outer entanglements,
Dwell not in the inner Void;
Be serene in the oneness of things,
And dualism vanishes by itself.

The Great Way
is calm and large-hearted,
For it nothing is easy,
nothing hard;
Small views are irresolute,
the more in haste,
the tardier they go.

It is one's own mind that
creates illusions.
Is this not the greatest
self-contradiction?

A special transmission outside the Scriptures;
No dependence on words and letters;
Direct pointing to the mind of man;
Seeing into one's own nature.

In the higher realm of true suchness,
There is neither 'self' nor 'other':
When direct identification is sought,
We can only say 'not two'.

You should know that so far
as Buddha-nature is concerned,
There is no difference between an
enlightened man and an ignorant one.
What makes the difference
is that one realizes it
And one doesn't.

Daily, nothing particular,
Only nodding to myself,
Nothing to choose, nothing to discard.
No coming, no going,
No person in purple,
Blue mountains without a speck of dust.
I exercise occult and subtle power,
Carrying water, shouldering firewood.

My way is through
mind-awakening.
How can it be conveyed in words?
Speech only produces some effect
when it falls on the uninstructed
ears of children.

The pure mind, the source of everything, shines forever and on all with the brilliance of its own perfection.
But the people of the world do not awaken to it, regarding only that which one sees, hears, feels and knows as mind.
Blinded by their own sight, hearing, feeling, knowing, they do not perceive the spiritual brilliance of the source-substance.

Do you see that Zen student?
He has forgotten what he has learned;
Yet he practises easily and freely
what he has learned
and also what he should learn.

A Zen student walks in Zen and sits in Zen
Whether in speech and action, or silence
or inaction,
His body dwells in peace.
He smiles at the sword that takes his life.
He keeps his poise even in the moment of death.

If you clearly realize for yourself that your mind does not abide anywhere whatsoever, That is called clearly perceiving your real mind. It is also called clearly perceiving reality. Only the mind which abides nowhere is the mind of a Buddha. It can be described as a mind set free.

There's a reality even prior to Heaven and Earth;
Indeed it has no form, much less a name;
Eyes fail to see it;
It has no voice for ears to detect.
To call it mind or Buddha violates its nature.
Absolutely quiet, and yet illuminating
It allows itself to be perceived only by the clear-eyed.
It is Dharma beyond form and sound;
It is Tao without words.
Wishing to entice the blind,
The Buddha has playfully let words escape
his golden mouth;
Heaven and Earth are ever since filled
with entangling briars.

The spring flowers, the autumn moon;
Summer breezes, winter snow.
If useless things do not clutter your mind,
You have the best days of your life.

Good friends, how then are
meditation and wisdom alike?
They are like the lamp and the light it gives forth.
If there is a lamp, there is light;
if there is no lamp, there is no light.
The lamp is the substance of light;
The light is the function of the lamp.
Thus, although they have two names,
In substance they are not two.
Meditation and wisdom are also like this.

Two come about because of one,
But don't cling to the one either!
So long as the mind does not stir,
The ten thousand things stay blameless;
No blame, no phenomena,
No stirring, no mind.

There is no special teaching:
The most ordinary things in our daily life
hide some deep meaning that is yet
most plain and explicit;
only our eyes need to see
where there is a meaning.

The perfect way is without difficulty,
save that it avoids picking and choosing.
Only when you stop liking and disliking
will all be clearly understood.

Without looking forward to tomorrow
every moment,
You must think only of this day and this hour.
Because tomorrow is difficult and unfixed
and difficult to know,
You must think of living the Buddhist way
whilst you live today.

The great mistake in swordsmanship
Is to anticipate the outcome of the engagement;
You ought not to be thinking of whether it ends
in victory or defeat.
Just let Nature take its course
And your sword will strike at the right moment.

Zen never leaves this world of facts.
Zen always lives in the midst of realities.
It is not for Zen to stand apart or keep itself away
From a world of names and forms.

When, just as they are,
white dewdrops gather
on scarlet maple leaves,
regard the scarlet beads.

Small views are full of foxy fears;
the faster, the slower.
When we attach ourselves to the idea
of enlightenment,
we lose our balance;
We infallibly enter the crooked way.
When we are not attached to anything,
all things are as they are;
With Activity there is no going or staying.
Obeying our nature, we are in accord with the Way,
wandering freely, without annoyance.

The breezes of spring
are blowing the ripples astray
along the water –
Today they will surely melt
the sheet of ice on the pond.

The cries of the insects
are buried at the roots of sparse pampas grass –
The end of Autumn
is in the colour of the last leaves.

Not twice this day
inch time foot gem.
This day will not come again.
Each minute is worth a priceless gem.

High, high from the summit of the peak,
Whatever way I look, no limit in sight!
No one knows I am sitting here alone.
A solitary moon shines in the cold spring.
Here in the spring – this is not the moon.
The moon is where it always is – in the sky above.
And though I sing this one little song,
In the song there is no Zen.

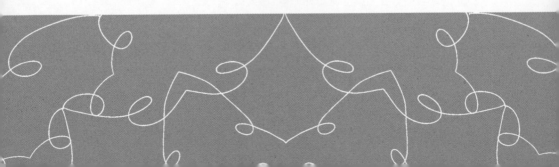

Walking is Zen, sitting is Zen,
Whether talking or remaining silent,
Whether moving or standing quiet,
The essence itself is ever at ease;
Even when greeted with swords and spears,
It never loses its quiet way,
So with poisonous drugs,
They fail to perturb its serenity.

You must concentrate on Zen practice
without wasting time,
thinking that there is only this day and this hour.
After that it becomes truly easy.
You must forget about the good and the bad
of your nature,
the strength or weakness of your power.

Our original Buddha-Nature is, in the highest truth,
devoid of any atom of objectivity.
It is void, omnipresent, silent, pure;
it is glorious and mysterious peaceful joy –
and that is all.
Enter deeply into it by awakening to it yourself.
That which is before you is it, in all its fullness,
utterly complete.
There is naught beside.

The stars on the pond.
Again the winter shower
ruffles the water.

I obtained not the least
thing from unexcelled,
complete awakening
And for this reason
it is called 'unexcelled,
complete awakening'.

Mind, an unruffled pool.
A thunderbolt!
My middle eye shot wide, revealing –
my ordinary self.

If a person knows the Tathagata,
Discerning nothing exists in him,
And knows all elements are extinct,
That man will swiftly become a Buddha.

The perfect way
knows no difficulties
Except that it refuses
to make preferences;
Only when freed
from hate and love,
It reveals itself fully
and without disguise.

If, at all times and in all places,
we steadily keep our thoughts free from foolish desire,
and act wisely on all occasions,
then we are practising wisdom.
One foolish notion is enough to shut off wisdom,
while one wise thought will bring it forth again.

But if a man speaks and acts by good mind, happiness follows him as a man's shadow. Those who act in evil, selfish ways suffer not only from the natural consequences of the acts, but are followed by the thought, 'I have done wrong,' and the memory of the act is stored in *karma* to work out its inevitable retribution in following lives.

In the landscape of spring
there is neither high nor low;
The flowering branches
grow naturally,
some long, some short.

The mirror is clear
and reflects anything that comes before it
and yet an image sticks to the mirror.
The Buddha-mind (the real, unborn mind)
is ten thousand times more clear than a mirror
and more inexpressibly marvellous.
In its light all such thoughts vanish without trace.
If you put your faith in this way of understanding,
however strongly such thoughts may arise
they do no harm.

For people,
life is a succession
of grasping and attachments,
and then, because of it,
they must assume the illusion
of pain and suffering.

Seeking the mind with the mind –
is not this the greatest of all mistakes?
Illusion produces rest and motion;
Illumination destroys liking and disliking.
All these pairs of opposites are created
by our own folly.
Dreams, delusions, flowers of air –
Why are we so anxious to have them in our grasp?
Profit and loss, right and wrong,
Away with them once and for all!

The mind, like a mirror,
is brightly illuminating and knows
no obstructions,
It penetrates the vast universe
to its minutest crevices;
All its contents, multitudinous in form,
are reflected in the mind,
Which, shining like a perfect gem,
has no surface, nor an inside.

With the evening breeze,
the water laps against
the heron's legs.

My hut in spring:
True, there is nothing in it –
there is everything.

If an eye never falls asleep,
all dreams will by themselves cease;
If the mind retains its absoluteness,
the ten thousand things are of one Suchness.

At the north window,

icy draughts whistle through the cracks,

At the south pond, wild geese huddle in snowy reeds,

Above, the mountain moon is pinched thin with cold,

Freezing clouds threaten to plunge from the sky.

Buddhas might descend to this world by the thousand,

They couldn't add or subtract one thing.

There is here, not there.
Infinity is before our eyes.

One in all, all in one –
if only this were realized,
no more worry about you
not being perfect.

Eaten by a cat!
Perhaps the cricket's widow
is bewailing that.

One moonlit night, the nun Chiyono was carrying
water in an old pail bound with bamboo.
The bamboo broke and the bottom fell out of the pail
and, at that moment, Chiyono was set free!
She wrote:
'No more water in the pail!
No more moon in the water!'

This is the barrier
where people come and people go
exchanging farewells;
For friends and strangers alike
this is the meeting barrier.

Why, it's but the motion
of eyes and brows!
And here I've been seeking it
far and wide.
Awakened at last,
I find the moon above the pines,
the river surging high.

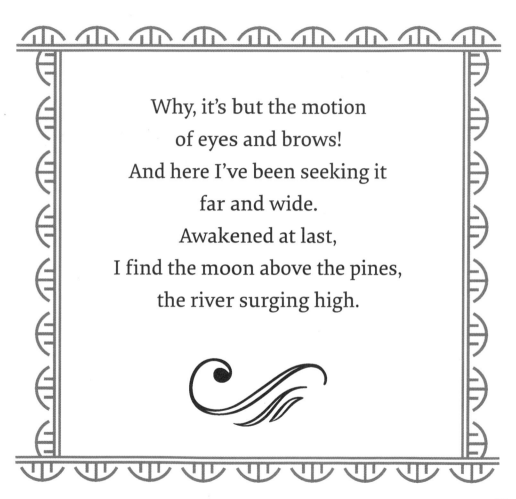

When the deep mystery
of one suchness is fathomed,
all of a sudden we forget
the external entanglements;
When ten thousand things
are viewed in their oneness,
we return to the origin
and remain where we have
ever been.

Infinitely small things are as
large as large things can be,
for here no external conditions
obtain;
infinitely large things are
as small as small things can be,
for objective limits
are here of no consideration.

The morning glory
which blooms for an hour
differs not in heart
from the giant pine,
which lives for a thousand years.

You should study not only
that you become a mother
when your child is born,
but also that you become
a child.

Everything is mind-made
and has no significance apart from mind.
As people come to understand this fact,
they are able to remove all delusions
and there is an end to all
mental disturbances forever.

Mountains and plains,
all are taken by the snow –
nothing remains.

In being 'not two' all is the same,
all that is comprehended in it;
the wise in the ten quarters,
they all enter into this
absolute reason.

Look upon the body as unreal,
an image in a mirror,
reflection of the moon in water.
Contemplate the mind as formless
yet bright and pure.

Like the empty sky it has no boundaries,
Yet it is right in this place, ever profound and clear.
When you seek to know it, you cannot see it.
You cannot take hold of it, but you cannot lose it.
In not being able to get it, you get it.
When you are silent, it speaks;
When you speak, it is silent.
The great gate is open to bestow alms,
And no crowd is blocking the way.

Energize your spirit
without becoming attached
to form or formlessness.

Zen doctrine is no subject for sentiment.

Doubts cannot be cleared by argument.

I stubbornly demand your silence

to save you from the pitfall

of being and non-being.

A dog and Buddha-nature?
The answer is in the question.
If you think of it in terms of duality,
you lose both body and life.

The ultimate end of things
is not bound by rules and measures;
In the mind harmonious
we have the principle of identity,
in which we find all strivings quieted;
Doubts and irresolutions
are completely done away with,
and the right faith is straightened;
There is nothing retained;
all is void, lucid, and self-illuminating,
there is no waste of energy –
This is where thinking never attains,
This is where the imagination fails to measure.

On the moor:
from things detached completely –
how the skylark sings.

When we stop movement, there is no-movement.
When we stop resting, there is no-rest.
When both cease to be, how can the unity subsist?
Things are ultimately, in their finality,
subject to no law.
For the accordant mind in its unity,
individual activity ceases.
All doubts are cleared up, true faith is confirmed.
Nothing remains behind;
there is not anything we must remember.

What is, is not, what is not, is.
Until you have grasped this fact,
your position is simply untenable.
One thing is all things;
all things are one thing.

Nothing whatever
is hidden;
From of old,
all is as clear
as daylight.

In the dark forest
a berry drops:
The sound of water.

When the mind is like wood or stone,
there is nothing to be discriminated.

One stroke has made me forget
all my previous knowledge,
No artificial discipline is at all needed;
In every movement I uphold the ancient way,
And never fall into the rut of mere quietism;
Wherever I walk no traces are left,
And my senses are not fettered by rules of conduct;
Everywhere those who have attained to the truth,
All declare this to be of highest order.

A sudden
light gleam:
off in the darkness
goes the night,
the heron's scream.

Unfettered at last, a travelling monk,
I pass the old Zen barrier.
Mine is a traceless stream-and-cloud life,
of these mountains,
which shall be my home?

On Mount Wu-t'ai
the clouds are steaming rice;
Before the ancient
Buddha hall,
dogs piss at heaven.

One Nature, perfect and pervading,
circulates in all natures;
One Reality, all-comprehensive,
contains within itself all realities;
The one Moon reflects itself
wherever there is a sheet of water.
And all the moons in the waters
are embraced within the one Moon;
The Dharma-body of all Buddhas
enters into my own being,
And my own being is found
in union with theirs.

This Mind-essence is variously characterized as something original, mysterious, mysteriously bright, illuminating, true, perfect, clear as a jewel.
It is not to be confused with our empirical mind, for it is not an object of thought.

One word settles heaven
and earth;
One sword levels
the whole world.

Empty, lucid, self-illuminated,
with no over-exertion
of the power of the mind.
This is where thought is useless.
This is what knowledge cannot fathom.

Wisdom does not vary with different persons;
What makes the difference is whether one's mind
is enlightened or deluded.
He who does not know his own essence of mind
and is under the illusion that Buddhahood can be
attained by outward religious rites is called slow-witted.

Baso was once asked by a monk,
'What is Buddha?'
He replied, 'There is no mind,
no Buddha.'

In the dense mist,
what is being shouted
between hill and boat?

The morality-jewel inherent in the Buddha-nature
stamps itself on the mind-ground
of the enlightened one; whose robe is cut out of mists,
clouds, and dews,
whose bowl anciently pacified the fiery dragons,
and whose staff once separated the fighting tigers;
listen now to the golden rings of his staff
giving out mellifluous tunes.
These are not mere symbolic expressions
devoid of historical contents;
Wherever the holy staff of Tathagatahood moves,
the traces are distinctly marked.

Sixty-six times have these eyes beheld
the changing scene of autumn,
I have had enough about moonlight,
Ask no more,
Only listen to the voice of pines and cedars
when no wind stirs.

Our original nature ... is pure being,
which is the source of everything and which
appears as sentient beings or as Buddhas,
As the rivers and mountains of the world
which have form,
As that which is formless or, as penetrating the
whole universe, is absolutely without distinctions:
There being no such entities as self and others.

The Way is perfect, like vast space, where nothing is lacking and nothing is in excess. Indeed, it is due to our choosing to accept or reject that we do not see the true nature of things. Live neither in the entanglement of outer things, nor in inner feelings of emptiness. Be serene in the oneness of things and such erroneous views will disappear by themselves.

There is no place to seek the mind;
it is like the footprints of the birds
in the sky.

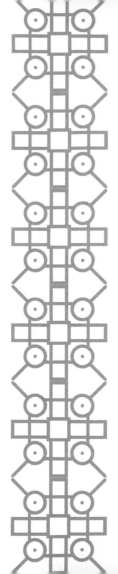

He neither seeks the true
nor severs himself from
the defiled,
He clearly perceives
that dualities are empty
and have no reality,
That to have no reality
means not to be one-sided,
neither empty
nor not-empty,
For this is the genuine form
of Tathagatahood.

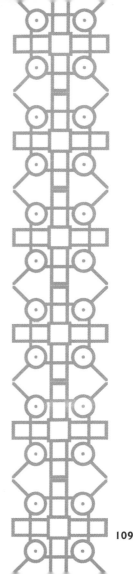

Winter desolation;
in the rainwater tub,
sparrows are walking.

Body clothed
in no-cloth robe,
Feet clad in turtle fur boots,
I seize my bow
of rabbit horn
And prepare to shoot
the devil Ignorance.

In nothingness of man I delight,
And, of all being, a thousand worlds
complete in my little cage.
I forget sin, demolish my heart,
and in enlightenment rejoice;
Who tells me that the fallen suffer in Hell's bonds?

Fathomed at last!
Oceans dried. Void burst.
Without an obstacle in sight,
it's everywhere!

But that the essence is there, is evident from the fact
that the eye sees, the ear hears and the mind thinks.
Only it is not discoverable as an individual object
or idea, objective or subjective;
for it has no existence in the way we talk of a tree
or a sun, of a virtue or a thought.

The fundamental
delusion of humanity
is to suppose that
I am here and
you are out there.

There is a reality even prior to Heaven and Earth;
Indeed, it has no form, much less a name;
Eyes fail to see it; it has no voice for ears to detect;
To call it Mind or Buddha would violate its nature,
For it then becomes like a visionary flower in the air;
It is not Mind, nor Buddha.

Learned audience, those who recite the word 'wisdom' the whole day long do not seem to know that wisdom is inherent in their own nature. But mere talking of food will not appease hunger, and this is exactly the case with these people.

A fallen blossom
returning to the bough,
I thought –
But no, a butterfly.

Because we are running after objects,
we lose track of the original mind and are tormented
by the threatening objective world, regarding it
as good or bad, true or false, agreeable or disagreeable.
We are thus slaves of things and circumstances.
The Buddha advised that our real position ought
to be exactly the opposite. Let things follow us and
await our commands. Let the true self give directions
in all of our dealings with the world.

Leaves falling,
lie on one
another;
the rain beats
on the rain.

Like a sword that cuts,
but cannot cut itself;
Like an eye that sees,
but cannot see itself.

Though numbers of *sutras* be plundered of their contents, success will never be attained. By looking into inner understanding, enlightenment will be realized in a flash of thought.

Human mind on its highest level is universal mind.
As universal mind, it is pure, tranquil, unconditioned,
in its true essential nature,
but because of its relations with the lower minds,
it becomes the storage for their reactions.

The secret of seeing things as they are
is to take off our coloured spectacles.
That being-as-it-is, with nothing extraordinary
about it, nothing wonderful,
is the great wonder.
The ability to see things normally is no small thing;
to be really normal is unusual.
In that normality begins to bubble up inspiration.

If you don't believe,
just look at September,
look at October!
The yellow leaves
falling, falling,
to fill both mountain
and river.

The purpose of a fish-trap is to catch fish,
and when the fish are caught, the trap is forgotten.
The purpose of a rabbit snare is to catch rabbits.
When the rabbits are caught, the snare is forgotten.
The purpose of words is to convey ideas.
When the ideas are grasped, the words are forgotten.
Where can I find a man who has forgotten words?
He is the one I would like to talk to.

If the essence is anything of which we can make
any statements, either affirmative or negative,
it is no more the essence.
It is independent of all forms and ideas, and yet
we cannot speak of it as not dependent on them.
It is absolute emptiness, *sunyata*,
and for this very reason,
all things are possible in it.

To bird and butterfly
it is unknown, this
flower here:
the autumn sky.

Better emancipate your mind than your body;
when the mind is emancipated, the body is free,
when both body and mind are emancipated,
even gods and spirits ignore
worldly power.

The sea darkens;
the voices of the wild ducks
are faintly white.

If we watch the shore
while we are sailing in a boat,
we feel that the shore is moving.
But if we look nearer to the boat itself,
we know then that it is the boat
that moves.
When we regard the universe in confusion
of body and mind, we often get the
mistaken belief that our mind is constant.
But if we actually practise Zen and come
back to ourselves,
we see that this was wrong.

Men are afraid to empty their minds,
fearing to fall into the Void with nothing
to which they can cling.
They do not know that the Void is not really void,
but the realm of Dharma . . .
It cannot be looked for or sought,
comprehended by wisdom or knowledge,
explained in words,
contacted materially [objectively]
or reached by meritorious achievement.

If for one instant of thought we become impartial,
then sentient beings are themselves Buddha.
In our mind itself a Buddha exists,
our own Buddha is the true Buddha.

The illimitable void of the universe is capable of holding myriads of things of various shapes and forms, such as the sun, the moon, the stars, mountains, rivers, worlds, springs, rivulets, bushes, woods, good men, bad men, Dharmas pertaining to goodness or badness, Deva planes, hells, great oceans and all the mountains of Mahameru.

Space takes in all these, and so does the voidness of our nature. We say that the essence of mind is great because it embraces all things, since all things are within our nature.

Much talk, much worry,
and you're less than ever
able to face things.
Be done with talk,
and be done with worry,
And there's no place you
cannot pass through.

Abide not with dualism,
Carefully avoid pursuing it;
As soon as you have right and wrong,
Confusion ensues and mind is lost.

The wild geese do not intend
to cast their reflection;
The water has no mind
to receive their image.

The two exist because of the One,
But hold not even to this One;
When a mind is not disturbed,
The ten thousand things offer
no offence.

Things which are past are past.
Do not speculate about them.
When your mind cuts itself off from the past,
that is called having no past.
Future events have not taken place.
Do not desire to seek for them.
When your mind cuts itself off from the future
that is called having no future.
Present events are present.

How admirable, he who thinks not
'Life is fleeting',
when he sees the lightning!

This Absolute Reason is beyond quickening time
and extending space,
For it, one instant is ten thousand years;
Whether we see it or not,
it is manifest everywhere in all the ten quarters.

There is nothing difficult about the Great Way,
but avoid choosing!
Only when you neither love nor hate
does it appear in all clarity.
A hair's breadth of deviation from it,
and a deep gulf is set between heaven and earth.
If you want to get hold of what it looks like,
do not be for or against anything.
The conflict of longing and loathing –
this is the disease of the mind.
Not knowing the profound meaning of things,
we disturb our original peace of mind to no purpose.

Above, below and around you,
all is spontaneously existing,
for there is nowhere which is
outside the mind.

Just as a peaceful ocean becomes suddenly a tumult of waves because of some passing tempest, so the ocean of mind becomes stirred by tempests of delusion and the winds of *karma*.

You must clearly understand that this Way is the void which depends on nothing and is attached to nothing.
It is all-pervading, spotless beauty;
it is self-existent and uncreated Absolute.

A brushwood gate,
and for a lock –
this snail.

All these existences and conditions take place illusively in the mind-essence. It is this alone that eternally abides as Suchness: bright, illuminating, all-pervading and immovable.

In this essence of eternal truth, there is indeed neither coming nor going, neither becoming confused nor being enlightened, neither dying nor being born. It is absolutely unattainable and unexplainable by the intellect, for it lies beyond all the categories of thought.

Entering the forest
he moves not the grass.
Entering the water
he makes not a ripple.

The Way is perfect like unto vast space,
With nothing wanting, nothing superfluous:
It is indeed due to making choice
That its suchness is lost sight of.

The viewer disappears along with the scene,
the scene follows the viewer into oblivion,
for scene becomes scene only through the viewer,
viewer becomes viewer because of the scene.

There is no place in Buddhism
for using effort.
Just be ordinary and nothing special.
Relieve your bowels, pass water, put on
your clothes and eat your food.
When you are tired, go and lie down.
Ignorant people may laugh at me,
but the wise will understand.

A lonely hut on the
mountain-peak towering
above a thousand others;
One half is occupied by an
old monk and the other
by a cloud:
Last night it was stormy
and the cloud was blown
away;
After all, a cloud could not
equal the old man's
quiet way.

In the landscape of spring, there is neither high nor low;
the flowering branches grow naturally,
some long, some short.

Hundreds of spring flowers:
the autumnal moon;
A refreshing summer breeze;
winter snow;
Free your mind of all idle thoughts,
And for you how enjoyable every
season is!

I lay sick by the low window,
　　propped on a crooked bed,
and thought how orderly the universe is.
　　A white bird flew across the sky;
　　　and my mind rolled forth
　　　　ten thousand feet.

The mind that creates its surroundings is never free from their shadow; it remembers, fears and laments, not only the past but the present and the future because they have arisen out of ignorance and greed. It is out of ignorance and greed that the world of delusion starts, and the vast complex of co-ordinating causes and conditions exist within the mind and nowhere else.

The mind-essence is in itself
thoroughly pure
and all-pervading,
and in it this formula holds:
form is emptiness
and emptiness is form.
Rupam sunyata, sunyateva rupam.

Very soon they die –
but of that there is no sign
in the locust-cry.

O my good friends gathered here,
if you desire to listen to the thunderous voice
of the Way,
exhaust your words, empty your thoughts,
for then you may come to recognize
this one Essence.

This mind-essence reveals itself in accordance
with the thoughts and dispositions of all beings, in
response to their infinitely varied degrees
of knowledge, and also to their *karma*.
In spite of its being involved in the evolution
of a world of multiplicities,
the essence in itself never loses its original purity,
the brilliance of emptiness.

Above, below and around you
all is spontaneously existing,
for there is nowhere
which is outside the mind.

Direct your eye right inward,
and you'll find a thousand regions of your mind
yet undiscovered.
Travel them and be expert in home-cosmography.

The stream hides itself
in the grasses
of departing Autumn.

In Zen, one would say that the
completely enlightened being
no longer rests
on any external moral code,
but naturally does good
and refrains from doing evil,
out of the very depth
of the heart.

This mind is no mind of conceptual thought
and it is completely detached from form,
so Buddhas and sentient beings do not differ at all.
If you can only rid yourselves
of conceptual thought
you will accomplish everything.

To see the truth here is the end of Zen study.
Give a sword to a fencing-master,
do not give a poem to a man who is not a poet.
In conversation reveal one third,
never give out the whole.

I have locked the gate on a thousand peaks
to live here with clouds and birds.
All day I watch the hills
as clear winds fill the bamboo door.
A supper of pine flowers,
monk's robes of chestnut dye –
what dream does the world hold
to lure me from these dark slopes?

The Three Thousand Worlds
that step forward
with the light snow,
and the light snow that falls
in those Three Thousand Worlds.

In former times men's minds were sharp.
Upon hearing a single sentence,
they abandoned study and came to
be called 'the sages who, abandoning
learning, rest in spontaneity'.
In these days people only seek
to stuff themselves with knowledge
and deductions,
placing great reliance
on written explanations
and calling all this the practice.

Mind is like the void in which
there is no confusion or evil,
as when the sun wheels through it,
shining upon the four corners of the world.
For when the sun rises and illuminates
the whole earth the void
gains not in brilliance;
and when the sun sets
the void does not darken.

Refreshing, the wind against the waterfall
as the moon hangs,
a lantern, on the peak,
and the bamboo window glows.
In old age, mountains are more beautiful
than ever.
My resolve:
that these bones be purified by rocks.

The deluded person concentrates on Buddha
and wishes to be born in the other land;
the awakened person makes pure his own mind.
Therefore the Buddha said:
'In accordance with the purity of the mind,
the Buddha-land is pure.'

Truth cannot be increased or decreased;
an instantaneous thought
lasts a myriad years.
There is no here, no there;
infinity is before our eyes.

If the eye does not sleep,
all dreaming
ceases naturally.
If the mind
makes no
discriminations,
all things are
as they really are.

Not a mote in the light above,
Soul itself cannot offer such a view.
Though dawn's not come,
the cock is calling.
The phoenix, flower in beak,
welcomes spring.

Infinitely small things are as large
as large things can be,
for here no external conditions obtain;
infinitely large things are as small
as small things can be,
for objective limits
are here of no consideration.

Do not seek for the truth;
religiously avoid following it.
If there is the slightest trace of this and that,
the mind is lost in a maze of complexity.
Duality arises from unity –
but do not be attached to this unity.

The wise man does nothing;
the fool shackles himself.
The truth has no distinctions;
these come from our foolish clinging
to this and that.

Deluded, a Buddha is a sentient being;
awakened, a sentient being is a Buddha.
Ignorant, a Buddha is a sentient being;
With wisdom, a sentient being is a Buddha.

For long years,
a bird in a cage;
today,
flying along
with clouds.

With the lamp of word and discrimination
one must go beyond the word and discrimination
and enter upon the path of realization.

As you go from place to place,
if you regard each one as your home,
they will all be genuine,
for when circumstances come,
you must not try to change them.
Thus your usual habits of feeling,
which make *karma* for Five Hells,
will of themselves become
the Great Ocean of Liberation.

Like lightning it flashes
through the shadows,
severing the spring wind;
the God of Nothingness
bleeds, crimson streaming.
I tremble at the heights
of Mount Sumera;
I will dive,
I will leap into
the stem of a lotus.

You have always been at one with Buddha,
so do not pretend you can attain to oneness
by various practices.

When you hear me talking of the void, do not at once
fall into the idea of vacuity (because this involves the
heresy of the doctrine of annihilation).
It is of the utmost importance that we should not
fall into this idea, because when a man sits quietly
and keeps his mind blank he will reside in a state of
'voidness of indifference'.

There is neither self nor living beings;
also there is no defeat or ruin;
whoever obtains such knowledge as this
will accomplish supreme enlightenment.

To keep our mind free from defilement under all circumstances is called idea-lessness.

Our mind should stand aloof from circumstances, and on no account should we allow them to influence the function of our mind.

But it is a great mistake to suppress our mind from all thinking; for even if we succeed in getting rid of all thoughts, and die immediately thereafter, we shall be reincarnated elsewhere.

The body and its surroundings are all alike manifestations of the one mind, but as observed by the human eye they appear to be different and they are classified as 'observer' and as 'things observed'. But as nothing exists apart from mind, there can be no essential difference between subject and object.

If they put a stop to conceptual thought and forget their anxiety, the Buddha will appear before them, for this mind is the Buddha and the Buddha is all living beings. It is not the less for being manifested in ordinary beings, nor is it greater for being manifested as the Buddha.

When thoughts arise,
then do all things arise.
When thoughts vanish,
then do all things vanish.

My advice to those whose eyes
have not been opened to the truth –
leap from the net
and see how immense is the ocean.

There is only one reality,
neither to be realized
or attained.
To say 'I am able to
realize something'
or 'I am able to attain
something'
is to place yourself
among the arrogant.

Regarding all things, only understand
that there must be no attachment.
No attachment means that feelings
of hatred and love do not arise.

This is the reason why the swordsman is always advised to be free from the thought of death or from anxiety about the outcome of the combat. As long as there is any 'thought' of whatever nature, that will assuredly prove disastrous.

Wind subsiding,
the flowers still fall;
bird crying,
the mountain silence
deepens.

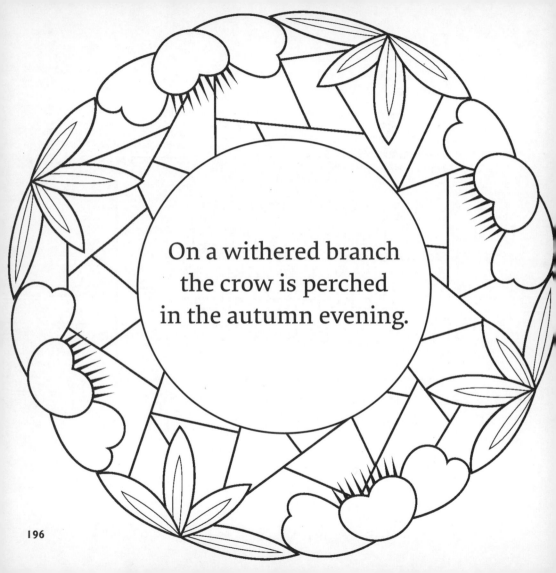

On a withered branch
the crow is perched
in the autumn evening.

When activity is stopped and passivity obtains,
This passivity is again the state of activity.
Remaining in movement or quiescence –
How shall we know the One?
Not thoroughly understanding the unity of the Way,
Both (activity and quiescence) are failures.
If you get rid of phenomena, all things are lost.
If you follow after the Void,
You turn your back on the selflessness of things.

Our Essence of Mind is
intrinsically pure,
and if we knew our mind
and realized what our
nature is,
all of us would attain
Buddhahood.

The infinitely small is as large
as the infinitely great;
For limits are non-existent things.
The infinitely large is as small
as the infinitely minute;
No eye can see their boundaries.

Things are things because of the mind;
The mind is the mind because of things.
If you wish to know what these two are,
They are originally one emptiness.
In this void, both mind and things are one,
All the myriad phenomena contained in both.

The tree is stripped,
all colour, fragrance gone,
yet already on the bough,
uncaring spring!

Whatever the great masters of Zen say, however they expound their teachings, of what use is all their learning and understanding to another person? That which gushes out from your own heart – that is what embraces heaven and earth.

A heavy snowfall disappears into the sea.
What silence!

That the self advances and confirms
the myriad things is called delusion.
That the myriad things advance and confirm
the self is called enlightenment.

Blue mountains are of themselves
blue mountains;
white clouds are of themselves
white clouds.

The sound of scouring
of the saucepan blends
with the tree frogs' voices.

When we use wisdom for introspection,
we are illumined within and without and in a position
to know our own mind. To know our mind is to
obtain liberation. To obtain liberation is to obtain
Samadhi of *prajna*, which is 'thoughtlessness'. What is
'thoughtlessness'? Thoughtlessness is to see all things
with a mind free from attachment. When in use,
it pervades everywhere yet sticks nowhere.

To study the Way is to study the self.

To study the self is to forget the self.

To forget the self is to be enlightened by all things.

To be enlightened by all things
is to remove the barriers between oneself
and others.

A village where they ring
no bells –
oh what do they do
at dusk in spring?

Do not keep perceptions nor abandon them nor cleave to them. Above, below and around you, all is spontaneous existing, for there is nowhere which is outside the Buddha-mind.

There a beggar goes!
Heaven and Earth he's wearing
for his summer clothes!

If we do not have
in ourselves
the Buddha mind,
then where are we
to seek Buddha?

Here one sees neither sin nor bliss,
neither loss nor gain;
In the midst of the Eternally Serene
no idle questionings are invited;
The dust of ignorance has been since of old
accumulating on the mirror never polished,
Now is the time once for all to see
the clearing positively done.

Clinging is never kept within bounds,
It is sure to go the wrong way;
Quit it, and things follow their own courses,
While the Essence neither departs nor abides.
Obey the nature of things, and you are in concord with
The Way, calm and easy, and free from annoyance;
but when your thoughts are tied,
you turn away from the truth,
They grow heavier and duller, and are not at all sound.

When we return to the root,
we gain the meaning;
When we pursue external objects,
we lose the reason.
The moment we are enlightened within,
We go beyond the voidness of a world
confronting us.

The activities of the mind have no limit
and form the surroundings of life.
An impure mind surrounds itself with impure
things and a pure mind surrounds itself with pure
surroundings, hence surroundings have no more limits
than the activities of the mind.

No offence offered,
and no ten thousand things;
No disturbance going,
and no mind set up to work;
The subject is quieted
when the object ceases,
The object ceases
when the subject is quieted.

The mind is the Buddha,
nor are there any other Buddhas or any
other mind. It is bright and spotless as the void,
having no form or appearance whatever.

There is nothing in the world that is not mind-created
and just as the human mind creates, the Buddha
creates, and all other beings act as Buddha acts.
So in the great task of creation, the human mind,
Buddha and all other beings are active alike.

It is doubt and unbelief that cause one to return
over and over again to the House of Birth
and Death; but through faith we enter into the
peace of the Eternal City called *Nirvana*.

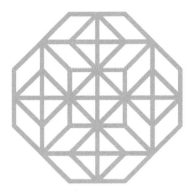

The object is an object for the subject,
The subject is a subject for the object;
Know that the relativity of the two
Rests ultimately on one Emptiness.

Transformations going on in an empty
world which confronts us
Appear real all because of Ignorance:
Try not to seek after the true,
Only cease to cherish opinions.

The ever-existent Buddha
is not a Buddha of stages.
Only awake to the one mind,
and there is nothing whatsoever
to be attained. This is the *real*
Buddha, and all sentient beings
are the one mind and
nothing else.

I have one jewel shining bright,
Long buried it was under
worldly worries;
This morning the dusty veil is off
and restored is its lustre,
Illuminating rivers and mountains
and ten thousand things.

A mind to search elsewhere
for the Buddha
is foolishness in the very
centre of foolishness.

My self of long ago,
In Nature non-existent;
Nowhere to go when dead,
Nothing at all.

Man is born many times, so he dies many times.

Life and death continue endlessly.

If he realizes the true meaning of unborn,

He will transcend both gladness and grief.

He lives in equanimity calmly and contentedly.
He is free of all care,
yet he acts naturally and reasonably.
He neither strives to avoid delusion
nor seeks after truth.
He knows delusions as baseless
and truth as himself.

Whoever can look at this earthly realm in every aspect without attachment, and likewise the Tathagat's body, this man will swiftly achieve Buddhahood.

If all things are to
be returned to the one,
to where is that one
to be returned?

Those who, reflecting within themselves,
Testify to the truth of self-nature,
To the truth that self-nature is no nature,
They have gone beyond all sophistry.
For them opens the gate of oneness of cause and effect,
And straight runs the path
of non-duality and non-trinity.

If a man with overall sameness
Conforms his mind to the Buddha doctrines
And enters the non-dual doctrine's gate
That man is difficult for thought to judge.

An unenlightened and bewildered life rises
out of a mind that is bewildered by its own creation
of a world of delusion outside of the mind.
When bewildered minds become clear
and cease to create impure surroundings,
they attain enlightenment.

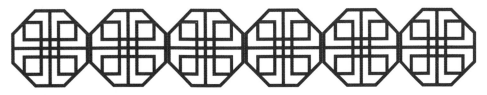

People grasp after things for their own imagined convenience and comfort; they grasp after wealth and treasure and honours; they cling desperately to life; they make arbitrary distinctions between good and bad, right and wrong, and then vehemently affirm and deny them.

To set up what you like against what you dislike,
that is disease of the mind:
when the deep meaning of the Way
is not understood,
peace of mind is disturbed to no purpose.

When oneness is not thoroughly understood,
In two ways loss is sustained:
The denying of reality is the asserting of it,
And the asserting of emptiness is the denying of it.

In my house there is a cave,
and in the cave there is nothing at all –
Pure and wonderfully empty,
resplendent with light like the sun,
A meal of greens will do for this old body,
A ragged coat will cover this phantom form.
Let a thousand saints appear before me –
I have the Buddha of Heavenly Truth!

Evil is born in the mind
and in the mind destroyed.

If you perceive both self and Buddhahood
as remaining in the sign of sameness,
then you will reside in no-residing
and be far beyond all things that exist.

How sad that
people ignore
the near and search
for truth afar.

Time flies quicker than an arrow
and life passes with greater transience
than the dew. However skilful you may be,
how can you ever recall a single day of the past?

All objects, all worlds, all facts in the world,
this body, this treasure, this dwelling,
are all appearances that have arisen
because of the activities of delusions
that are inherent within their own
mental appearances.

All things good or bad, beautiful or ugly,
should be treated as void.
Even in time of disputes and quarrels
we should treat our intimates
and our enemies alike
and never think of retaliation.

Yajnadatta, a citizen of Sravasti,
one morning looked into the mirror and found a face
with charming features. He thought his own head had
disappeared and thereby went crazy.
This story is used to illustrate the stupidity of clinging
to relative knowledge which arises from the opposition
of subject and object. As we cling to it as having
absolute value, a world of topsy-turviness extends
before us. The original bright and charming face
is ours only when we realize the fact by reflecting
within ourselves, instead of running after unrealities.

Over the river
the shining moon;
in the pine trees,
sighing wind;
all night long
so tranquil – why?
And for whom?

If one understands all the elements –
that nothing exists in the perceiver,
that perceived elements are
nothing, too –
then one can illuminate the world.

Here is a tree older than the forest itself;
The years of its life defy reckoning.
Its roots have seen the upheavals of hill and valley;
Its leaves have known the changes of wind and frost.
The world laughs at its shoddy exterior
And cares nothing for the fine grain of the wood inside.
Stripped free of flesh and hide,
All that remains is the core of truth.

Snow that we two
saw together –
this year
is it fallen anew?

You must concentrate on Zen practice without wasting time, thinking that there is only this day and this hour. After that it becomes truly easy. You must forget about the good or the bad of your nature, the strength and the weakness of your power.

He neither seeks the true nor severs himself
from the defiled,
He clearly perceives that dualities are empty
and have no reality,
That to have no reality means not to be
one-sided, neither empty nor not-empty,
For this is the genuine form
of Tathagatahood.

Whence is my life?
Whither does it go?
I sit alone in my hut and meditate quietly;
With all my thinking I know nowhere,
nor do I come to any whither:
such is my present,
Eternally changing – all in emptiness!
In this emptiness the ego rests for a while,
with it yeas and nays;
I know not where to place them,
I follow my *karma* as it moves, in perfect contentment.

Returning to the root, we get the essence;
Following after appearances, we lose the spirit.
If for only a moment, we see within,
we have surpassed the emptiness of things.
Changes that go on in this emptiness
all arise because of our ignorance.

All you have to do is
realize that birth and death, as
such, should not be avoided and
then they will cease to exist, for
if you can understand that birth
and death are *nirvana* itself, there
is not only no necessity to avoid
them but also nothing to search
for that is called *nirvana*.

Obey the nature of things,
and you are in concord with the Way,
Calm and easy and free from annoyance;
But when your thoughts are tied,
you turn away from the truth,
They grow heavier and duller and are not all sound.

The phenomena of light and dark alternate with each other, but the nature of the void remains unchanged. So it is with the Mind of the Buddha and of sentient beings. If you look upon the Buddha as presenting a pure, bright or enlightened appearance, or upon sentient beings as presenting a foul, dark or mortal-seeming appearance, these attachments to form will keep you from supreme knowledge, even after the passing of as many aeons as there are sands in the Ganges.

The ego-self and the idea of possession have no true existence. There is only the age-old habit of erroneous thinking that leads people to perceive and to discriminate various aspects of the world, where in reality there are none.

However deep one's knowledge of philosophy, it is like a piece of hair flying in space; however important one's experience in worldly things, it is like a drop of water thrown into an unfathomable abyss.

When you sit, sit;
when you walk, walk.
Above all, don't wobble.

Not a single thought arising,
empty yet perceptive,
still, yet illuminating,
complete like the Great Emptiness
containing all that is wonderful.

During the period before the world was manifested
there were no names. The moment the Buddha arrives
in the world there are names, so we clutch hold
of forms. In the great Tao there is absolutely nothing
secular or sacred. If there are names, everything
is classified in limits and bounds.

Keep your mind
alive and free without
abiding in anything
or anywhere.

Form and sensation
are without number
so are conception, thought and consciousness.
He who understands that is so,
that man is the great solitary saint.

The human mind discriminates itself
from the things that appear to be outside itself
without first realizing that it has first created these
very things within its own mind.
This has been going on from beginningless time
and the delusion has become firmly fixed
within the mind
and even adheres things to themselves.

Sleet falling;
fathomless,
infinite
loneliness.

Zen opens a man's eyes to the greatest mystery
as it is daily and hourly performed;
it enlarges the heart to embrace the eternity of time
and the infinity of space in its every palpitation;
it makes us live in the world
as if walking in the garden of Eden.

Among a thousand clouds
and ten thousand streams,
Here lives an idle man,
in the daytime wandering over green mountains,
At night coming home to sleep by the cliff.
Swiftly the springs and autumns pass,
But my mind is at peace, free from dust or delusion.
How pleasant to know I need nothing to lean on,
To be still as the waters of the autumn river.

If a person thinks true enlightenment
is release from the influxes,
and detachment from all things of
the world,
he does not possess the pure eye of truth.

When an artist draws
a picture, the details are
filled in from his own
mind and a single picture
is capable of an infinity of
detail; so the human mind
fills in the surroundings
of its life.

In Buddhism,
the un-born is the un-dying.
Life is a position of time.
Death is a position of time.
They are like winter and spring.
We do not consider that winter becomes
spring, or that spring becomes summer.

In the one he understands the countless.
In the countless he understands the one.
Evolving lives are not reality.
For the man who is wise there is no fear.

We sleep with both legs outstretched,
free of the true, free of the false.

If people can change their viewpoints, can break up these age-old habits of thinking, can rid their minds of desires and infatuations and egoism, then the wisdom of true enlightenment is possible.

No one can live your life except you.
No one can live my life except me.
You are responsible. I am responsible.
But what is our life? What is our death?

On a journey, ill –
and my dreams,
on withered fields
are wandering still.

Should you live for a hundred years just wasting your time, every day will be filled with sorrow; should you drift as the slave of your senses for a hundred years and yet live truly for only so much as a single day, you will in that one day not only live a hundred years of life, but also a hundred years of your future life.

Whoever perceives that all the Buddhas
Appear in the world in the same instant
And yet that nothing really arises
That person has a great reputation.

There is only one mind and not a particle of anything else on which to lay hold, for this mind is the Buddha. If you students of the Way do not awake to this mind substance, you will overlay mind with conceptual thought, you will seek the Buddha outside yourself, and you will remain attached to forms.

When mind and each
believing mind are not divided,
And undivided are each believing mind
and Mind,
This is where words fail;
For it is not of the past, present
and future.

The long night;
the sound of water
says what I think.

Like the clear stillness of autumn water – pure and without activity; in its tranquil depths are no obstructions. Such a one is called a man of Tao, also a man who has nothing further to do.

The ignorant cherish the idea of rest
and unrest,
the unenlightened have likes and dislikes.

No one lives at the Barrier of Fuha;
the wooden penthouse is fallen away;
all that remains
is the autumn wind.

All things being empty, so is the mind.

As the mind is empty, all is.

My mind is not divisible: all is contained in my every thought which appears as enlightenment to the wise, illusion to the stupid. Yet enlightenment and illusion are one. Do away with both, but don't remain 'in between' either. In this way you will be emptiness itself which, stainless and devoid of the interrelationships of things, transcends realization. In this way the true Zen priest commonly conducts himself.

Scoop up the water and the moon
is in your hands;
hold the flowers and your clothes
are scented with them.

To save life
it must be destroyed;
when utterly destroyed,
one dwells for the first time
in peace.

In the true essence there is neither *samskrita* (created) nor *asamkrita* (uncreated); they are like *maya* or flowers born of hallucination. When you attempt to manifest what is true by means of what is erroneous, you make both untrue. When you endeavour to explain object by subject and subject by object, you create a world of endless opposites; nothing real is grasped. To experience perfect interfusion, let all the opposites be dissolved. When there is clinging of any sort, and an ego-mind is asserted, the essence dissipates and the mysterious lotus fades.

The skylark:
its voice alone fell
leaving nothing behind.

In the deep mystery of this 'Things as they are',
We are released from our relations to them.
When all things are seen 'with equal mind',
They return to their nature.

When you are silent, it speaks;
When you speak, it is silent.
The great gate is wide open
to bestow alms,
And no crowd
is blocking the way.

Heaven and Earth
and I are of the same
root, the ten-thousand
things and I
are of one substance.

The doctrine of fearlessness is taught
as loudly as a lion roars:
What a pity that confused minds,
inflexibly hardened like leather,
Understand only that grave offences
are obstructions to Enlightenment,
And are unable to see into the secrets
of the Tathagata's teaching.

Do not build up your views on your senses and thoughts, do not carry on your understanding based on your senses and thoughts; but at the same time do not seek the mind away from your senses and thoughts, do not grasp the *Dharma* by rejecting your senses and thoughts. When you are neither attached to nor detached from them, when you are neither abiding with nor clinging to them, then you enjoy your perfect unobstructed freedom, then you have your seat of enlightenment.

Both delusion and enlightenment
originate in the mind,
and every fact arises
from the activities of the mind
just as different things arise
from the sleeve of the magician.

Without enlightenment there would be no difference
between a Buddha and other living beings;
while a gleam of enlightenment is enough to make
any living being the equal of a Buddha.
Since all *dharmas* are immanent in our mind,
there is no reason why we should not realize
intuitively the real nature of suchness.

The wind brings
fallen leaves enough
to make a fire.

My mind is like the autumn moon
Shining clean and clear in the green pool.
No, that's not a good comparison.
Tell me, how shall I explain?

Zen enlightenment is as if you have been far away from home for many years, when you suddenly see your father in town. You know him right away without a doubt. There is no need to ask whether he is your father or not.

When in Zen there is the advice to give up all concepts, it must of course include the concept of no concept.

Awakening is where there is no birth, no extinction; it is seeing into the state of Suchness, absolutely transcending all the categories of constructed mind.

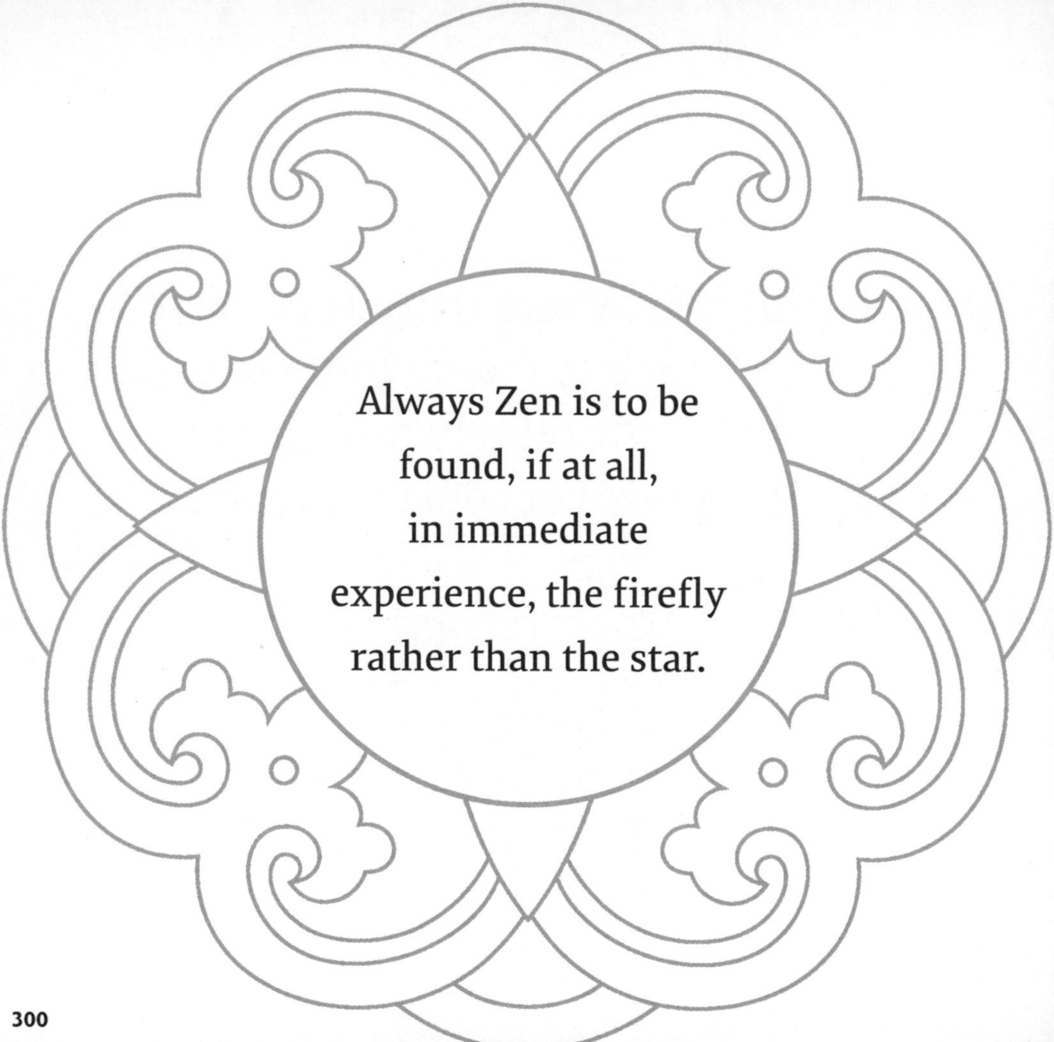

Always Zen is to be
found, if at all,
in immediate
experience, the firefly
rather than the star.

Suppose a warrior, forgetting that he was already wearing his pearl on his forehead, were to seek for it elsewhere, he could travel the whole world without finding it. But if someone who knew what was wrong were to point to him, the warrior would immediately realize that the pearl had been there all the time.

The old pine tree speaks
divine wisdom;
the secret bird manifests
eternal truth.

For when you have really heard the sound of rain,
you can hear, and see, and feel everything else
in the same way – as needing no translation,
as being just that which it is,
though it may be impossible to say what.

A man is not called wise because he talks and talks again; but if he is peaceful, loving and fearless, then he is in truth called wise.

When a bird is alive, it eats ants.

When the bird is dead, ants eat the bird.

Time and circumstances can change at any time.

Don't devalue or hurt anyone in life.

You may be powerful today – but remember –

Time is more powerful than you.

One tree makes a million matchsticks,

Only one matchstick is needed to burn a million trees.

Whatever precious jewel there is in the heavenly worlds, there is nothing comparable to one who is Awakened.

Everything is continuously changing.
Life is like a river flowing on and on, ever-changing.
Sometimes it flows slowly and sometimes swiftly.
It is smooth and gentle is some places, but later on
snags and rocks crop up out of nowhere.
As soon as we think we are safe,
something unexpected happens.

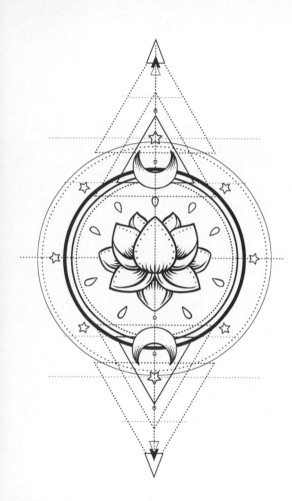

Never stop
learning,
because life
never stops
teaching.

To enjoy good health, to bring true happiness to one's family, to bring peace to all, one must first discipline and control one's own mind. If a man can control his mind, he can find the way to Enlightenment, and all wisdom and virtue will naturally come to him.

Flow with whatever
may happen, and let your
mind be free:
stay centred by accepting
whatever you are doing.
This is the ultimate.

To practice Zen or the Martial Arts, you must live
intensely, wholeheartedly, without reserve –
as if you might die in the next instant.

All love is expansion, all selfishness is contraction.
Love is therefore the only law of life.
He who loves lives, he who is selfish is dying.
Therefore love for love's sake, because it is the only
law of life, just as you breathe to live.

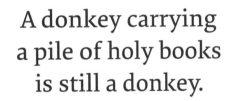

A donkey carrying
a pile of holy books
is still a donkey.

The clear water
sparkles like crystal.
You can see through it easily,
right to the bottom.
My mind is free
from every thought,
Nothing in the myriad
realms can move it.

Make an island of yourself,
make yourself your refuge;
there is no other refuge.
Make truth your island, make truth your refuge;
there is no other refuge.

Can you polish your mysterious mirror
And leave no blemish?

A man of great will carries with him a sword of Prajna,
Whose flaming Vajra-blade cuts all the entanglements
of knowledge and ignorance;
It not only smashes in pieces the intellect
of the philosophers
But disheartens the spirit of the evil ones.

All my past achievements have been efforts vainly
and wrongly applied. I realize it fully now,
I have been a vagrant monk for many years
to no end whatever.

Words!
The Way is beyond language,
For in it there is
No yesterday
No tomorrow
No today.

The thief left it behind –
the moon at the window.